THE
GHOSTLY TALES
OF
LONG ISLAND

Published by Arcadia Children's Books
A Division of Arcadia Publishing
Charleston, SC
www.arcadiapublishing.com

Spooky America is a trademark of Arcadia Publishing, Inc.

First published 2020

Manufactured in the United States

ISBN 978-1-4671-9805-9

Library of Congress Control Number: 2020938907

Photo credits: used throughout Eugenia Petrovskaya/Shutterstock.com; Nataliia K/
Shutterstock.com; In-Finity/Shutterstock.com; vectorkuro/Shutterstock.com; p. iv-v
Neural Networks/Shutterstock.com; the Hornbills Studio/Shutterstock.com; Caso
Alfonso/Shutterstock.com; Ivakoleva/Shutterstock.com; LDDesign/Shutterstock.com;
p. vi, 10, 30, 44, 66, 78, 94 andreiuc88/Shutterstock.com; p. 3 Forgem/
Shutterstock.com; p. 4, 36, 72, 100 welburnstuart/Shutterstock.com; p. 18, 50, 84
Solid photos/Shutterstock.com; p. 20 Zina Seletskaya/Shutterstock.com; p. 24, 60, 90
Christian Mueller/Shutterstock.com; p. 29 KsanaGraphica/Shutterstock.com; p. 38,
70 Cattallina/Shutterstock.com; p. 43 CHAIWATPHOTOS/Shutterstock.com; p. 54-55
Nosyrevy/Shutterstock.com; p. 58, 75 VladimirCeresnak/Shutterstock.com; p. 62-63
Pavel Kovaricek/Shutterstock.com; p. 64 PHEANGPHOR studio/Shutterstock.com; p. 83
Elena Paletskaya/Shutterstock.com.

Spooky America

THE
GHOSTLY TALES
OF
LONG ISLAND

RACHEL KEMPSTER BARRY

Adapted from *Historic Haunts of Long Island* by Kerriann Flanagan Brosky with Joe Giaquinto

ARCADIA
PUBLISHING

NEW
YORK

CONNECTICUT

3

9

13

8

10

16

1

4

11

6

2

15

12

7

LONG ISLAND

5

ATLANTIC OCEAN

RHODE
ISLAND

MASSACHUSETTS

TABLE OF CONTENTS MAP KEY

Introduction

Growing up on Long Island, I never realized how much history surrounded us. And with history comes tales of murder, pirates, spies, hauntings, and ghosts! From lighthouses to creaky old homes to mansions to bakeries, Long Island is full of fascinating and haunting tales that you'll read about in the pages that follow—if you're brave enough. You're brave enough, right?

Now perhaps you're the kind of reader who doesn't believe in ghosts. You think they're the stuff of movies and novels and imagination. That's okay! Even if you're not a believer in the supernatural, you'll find plenty of spooky stories in Long Island's history to keep you up late at night. There's Revolutionary War intrigue, looting pirates, hidden rooms inside elaborate mansions, and secret cemeteries.

If you do believe in ghosts, then you'll find lots of eyewitness accounts from people of all ages who claim to have seen, heard, or felt the presence of spirits. You'll start to notice patterns too. Ever walk through an old building when you feel a sudden drop in temperature? That might be a spirit trying to say hello. Ghosts also have a habit of knocking things over like books and papers and teacups. (This might be an excellent excuse to use next time you get in trouble for making a mess—a ghost did it!) And did you know a ghostly vortex is what you call a space where ghosts can freely move from world to world? It's true, according to professional ghost hunters.

These tales remind ghost fans and disbelievers alike that history can't be stopped. What happened three hundred years ago or twenty years ago stays with us now and forever. The more we learn (why did people leave tiny shoes under the floorboards?), the more secrets we uncover (Long Island had its very own spy ring!), and the more we can understand who we were then, who we are today, and who we'll be in the future. And there's nothing scary about that.

The Fiorello Dolce Bakery

Think of all the wonderful things you can find in a bakery: giant cookies, fudgy brownies, chocolate cakes—and sometimes, GHOSTS!

At the Fiorello Dolce Bakery in Huntington, the bakery's owner and chef, Gerard Fiorvanti, believes he has a haunting on his hands. Could it be true?

Here's a question: does a bakery ghost have a sweet tooth? Does it ever stick its ghost-fingers in the frosting? We might never know the answers to those questions, but if we take a look back, we can understand why some ghosts chose *this* bakery.

In the 1900s, there were row houses in the area where Fiorello Dolce Bakery now sits. Row houses are houses that share walls with their neighbors. Imagine a very long house separated so that each family had a slice of the house to call their own. For many years, these particular row houses were home to poor workers and had fallen into bad condition.

In the early 1970s, the row houses were demolished to make space for parking lots and businesses—but they didn't get rid of everything. The ghost of Eddie, a man rumored to have died outside the row houses, stuck around. Chef Gerard is certain that Eddie visits him from time to time. He's a relatively quiet ghost, and he's also the oldest ghost at the bakery.

Yes. There's more than one ghost at the bakery. According to the chef, the bakery has always had many incredible ghost visitors who cause all sorts of mischief for him and the staff.

"Gerard. . . Gerard. . . Gerard. . ." One of the ghosts likes to whisper Chef Gerard's name late at night or early in the morning when there's no one else at the bakery. Spooky, right? What would you do if a ghost called your name? Run? Answer back?

More mischief happens during the night when the bakery lights go out. Pastry carts move on their own, oven doors slam closed, paper towels unfurl, and buckets mysteriously fly off shelves. In the morning, Chef Gerard and the other bakers find these ghostly surprises. For the chef, there's no other explanation: when left alone in the bakery, the resident ghosts like to make a mess.

Turns out that the chef thinks that some of those mischievous ghosts are his friends and family members. "Aunt Angie, who passed away ten years ago. . . . She's always here at the bakery with my grandmother, taking care of the front of the store and keeping customers out of the kitchen," he says. He also believes that one ghost, Charlie, is the bakery's landlord who died several years back at the age of 92.

When Charlie was alive, he absolutely loved the bakery and visited whenever he could. He enjoyed the pastries almost as much as he loved showing Chef Gerard a better way to make them. He'd say to the chef, "Oh, let me tell you how to make it." This drove the chef a little crazy, but he still loved getting visits from Charlie. And he still does, even now that Charlie's a ghost.

"I think Charlie is responsible for all the little things that are happening in the bakery kitchen— when a knife falls and slides across the table, when the spatulas rattle, when the rolling rack moves, when the parchment paper comes flying out of its compartment, when the spoons fall," says Chef Gerard. It sure sounds like Charlie still loves showing the chef that he's the boss of the kitchen.

Chef Gerard isn't the only one who has had the luck (or misfortune?) of seeing and hearing the haunted residents of the bakery. Other members of the staff have had their own chilling encounters.

One day, Kristy, who helped run the bakery, went into the walk-in refrigerator to get supplies.

She heard someone whistle at her from inside the refrigerator. She ran out, terrified, and told her co-workers, "Someone just whistled at me!" It sounded so real (and loud!), but there was definitely no one else in there with her. She checked every corner for the sign of another person with no luck. Could it have been a ghost? Kristy thought it could be.

After a few minutes, she got up the courage and yelled back into the refrigerator, "Stop whistling at me!" She swears she heard a grunting sound in reply—and then the whistling stopped. The ghost listened. She never heard the whistling noise again.

With all of these hauntings, do customers stay away from the bakery? No way! The Fiorello Dolce Bakery still serves its customers every day. The customers don't care if it's haunted, so long as they can get their fill of its delicious sweet treats.

The Old Bethpage Village Restoration

OLD BETHPAGE

You can time travel at the Old Bethpage Village Restoration, a colonial farming village located in Nassau County. There, you'll be transported back to the 1800s, when candy cost a penny in the general store, blacksmiths forged horseshoes, and workers churned butter by hand. Keep walking the paths, and you'll see rows of sturdy homes that have stood for over one hundred years. Those homes were plucked from all over Long Island— from the North Fork to Smithtown to Woodbury to

Hempstead—and moved to the village in the late 1960s. When the Old Bethpage Village Restoration opened to the public in 1970, all the homes had been restored so visitors could see and experience what life was like for Long Island families in the nineteenth century.

But when the workers moved those houses, did they bring with them more than walls, windows, and doors? Could it be that the spirits of their former owners came along too? That's what people think. Let's look more closely at three of these houses: the Williams farmhouse, the Conklin house, and the Hewlett house.

The Williams family built their farmhouse in stages, from 1820 through 1850. It was originally located in New Hyde Park before being moved to the village. There, it was renovated and restored to look like it did in 1860. For the workers who run the museum and give tours to visitors, the house has been a source of many scares.

One day, workers were cleaning up the sitting

room, preparing for another day of visitors. As one woman started dusting off a fragile set of teacups, a voice called out, "Put my teacup down."

The worker was startled. Was someone playing a trick? She asked the other woman in the room, "Did you just say that?" Nope. The other worker hadn't said a thing. In fact, she was in another room when the ghostly command was made.

So who said it? Who didn't want her teacups disturbed?

Another time, someone was working on a project downstairs on the sewing table. Back in the 1860s, the owner of the house, Henry Williams, lived with this sister Ester. She was said to have spent most of her days working at that very sewing table. As the day went on, the woman working at the table heard noises upstairs. At first, the noises were easy to brush off. A subtle whoosh or bang could be explained away. Maybe the house was creaking or a squirrel was on the roof. As the hours passed, the sounds got louder and louder. Finally, it was too much to ignore, and she asked her co-worker to come with her to investigate the noise. What she found upstairs was chilling. While no one had been upstairs all day, the room was a mess! A trunk was open, and fabric was strewn about.

Could it be that Ester was angry that someone dared sit at her sewing table? Could it also have been Ester who had yelled about the teacup? Over the years, there have been other incidents: noises in the hallways, objects moved from room to room. Perhaps Ester wants to be left alone in her house, to sew in peace for all of eternity.

Toward the center of the village is another house plagued by mysterious happenings. The Conklin house was built in Smithtown around 1820. Its owner at the time, Thomas Hallock, had a tavern. One of his regular customers, Joseph, ended up marrying Hallock's niece, Thankful. (Yes, she was really named "Thankful.") She bought the house from her uncle, and Thankful and Joseph raised their two children in the home.

Some believe that those children haunt the

Conklin house to this day. On two different occasions, visitors to the village have seen a sad-looking little girl, around eight years old, near the house. One time she was sitting on the porch, and another time she was sitting on the front steps.

Inside the house, the hauntings continue. Many have heard the noise of children running around and playing on the home's second floor. Each time the staff assumes a group of children have gotten away from their parents or teachers, but when they reach the top of the steps, they can't find a single child. Are they just hearing things, or are the ghosts of Joseph and Thankful's children continuing to play in their former home?

One visitor saw the spirit of a man in the Conklin house too. She visited as a child when she spotted the man the first time. Years later, when she was 23 years old, she came back to the house again with her mother, to see if the man was still there.

HE WAS! Not only that, he communicated to her that he was upset that the house had been moved from its original spot. He wasn't an angry spirit, he just wasn't very happy with the new location of the house. Maybe he didn't like visitors coming in and out of his former home all day long.

Other visitors, including a second-grade boy on a school field trip, have spotted a ghostly woman roaming around the second floor. As the boy left the house, he asked the tour guide, "Who's the yucky lady upstairs?" Could that have been Thankful herself? Perhaps she was busy trying to quiet down her noisy ghostly children.

The final spooky stop on our tour of the Old Bethpage Village Restoration is the Hewlett house. The Hewlett house, named for the family who lived there, was moved to the village in 1968. Captain Charles Hewlett built his family's home in 1794 after returning from exile (which means he was sent away as punishment). Why was he exiled? Hewlett was a loyalist who fought alongside the British in the Revolutionary War. When the British lost, he was forced out of the country.

Hewlett eventually passed the family home to his son Lewis. The house, as it now stands has been restored to how it looked in the 1840s, when Lewis was master of the house. Lewis's wife died in 1840. But he continued to live in the house, with his younger sister and several servants.

When the Hewlett house first arrived at the village, security guards reported seeing a woman in white circling the house. One night, an alarm went off in the house, and one of the guards went to check it out. As he headed up the stairs, he heard two people talking downstairs. He knew he was alone, and when he walked through the darkened house, step by step, he could see that he was the only person inside. The talking stopped.

He ran for the front door to get out, but it was locked.

Thinking fast, he threw open a window and jumped through.

A few weeks later, when he came back inside the house, he once again heard a voice. This time, it was clearly a male voice. And it was laughing at him.

The Execution Rocks Lighthouse

KINGS POINT

Is the Execution Rocks Lighthouse the deadliest lighthouse of all? Located on a dangerously rocky reef a mile north of Sands Point, the abandoned Execution Rocks Lighthouse has a violent history.

What happened here, on these terrible rocks? (Murder.) Do the tormented souls of the murdered continue to visit the site of the rocks and lighthouse? (Quite possibly.)

The most commonly told tales about the Execution Rocks are from the American

Revolution. As the legend goes, during the Battle of Long Island, British soldiers rounded up American rebels. They planned to put them to death, but they wanted to do it quietly. They wanted to avoid riling up the American soldiers. Because the British had arrived by ship, they knew very well how to navigate the treacherous waters around Long Island. They also knew of a quiet spot—a rocky island in the middle of Long Island Sound—where they could take the prisoners. Once there, the British soldiers supposedly beat

the American rebels and then chained them to the rocks at low tide. As the tide came in slowly and steadily, the prisoners, with no hope of escape, drowned. Many became lunch for hungry sharks. Even worse, the British kept the bodies of the dead soldiers chained to the rocks as a terrifying warning and torment for future prisoners.

As the legend goes, the ghosts of the murdered prisoners haunt the rocks. Some even think they got their revenge when a ship full of British soldiers went down near the rocks, which killed everyone aboard.

With such a terrible history behind it, why did anyone decide to erect a lighthouse atop these deadly, murderous, potentially haunted rocks?

In 1847, under President Lincoln, plans were made to build the lighthouse. The keeper of the lighthouse was to live in the small circular room on the lowest floor, a tiny round space hardly suited for a home. Over the years, the space held several lighthouse keepers before a separate keepers' dwelling was built in 1868.

Once the lighthouse was built, the bad aura around the deadly place continued. The lighthouse survived two fires: one in 1918 and another in 1921. And in the winter of 1920, a steamer ship called *Maine* ran aground on the rocks due to snow, ice, high winds, and a full-moon tide. Accounts said the ship crashed stern first (the stern is the back of the boat) and nearly hit the lighthouse. Luckily, everyone on board survived, including 14 horses. The bad news? Because the weather was so terrible, it took three long days for the victims of the crash to be rescued. It was brutally cold on board, and there was constant fear that the ship would break apart. Then the lighthouse station's supply of drinking water ran out. For once, the terrible winter weather was helpful—they melted snow to drink and give to the horses.

Unlike other lighthouses, where keepers stay for decades, it's been said that the average time a lighthouse keeper would stay at Execution Rocks was only six months. Was it the weather? The tiny living conditions? Or the ghosts? In fact, keepers had an unusual contract: they were allowed to leave their position at any time. As their contract read, "No lighthouse keeper was to ever feel chained to the reef," an eerie reminder of the dark history of the rocks.

Today, the lighthouse has no keeper. It is closed and maintained by the US Coast Guard. But if it ever reopens, would you be brave enough to survive a spell as the keeper of the Execution Rocks Lighthouse?

St. James
General Store

St. James

You can find everything at the St. James General Store, from wooden toys to fudge to books to candles. If you're lucky (or unlucky?), you might also find a ghost or two wandering the floors.

Ebenezer Smith opened the store in 1857 after a successful visit out West. In the early 1850s, he heard about the California Gold Rush. Tempted by the promise of riches, he grabbed his mule and supplies and headed across the country to find gold. After a few years and some success, he returned to Long Island and opened the general store. Eventually, his son Everett Smith took over.

The store was an important place for everyone in the community. They could buy what they needed, from medicine to horse supplies to groceries. It was also the site of the first post office in town and the very first telephone. The townspeople could count on finding what they need—and catching up on local gossip—anytime they stopped in. In fact, the store was so central to life in town that all the parades kicked off right from the front porch.

The store hasn't changed much since 1894. The wood counters, flooring, potbelly stove, and tea canisters are all original.

In 1999, Karen Sheedy became the store's general manager. Her favorite thing about the St. James General Store? The smell. "There is a smell every so often that just reminds me of the quintessential general store," she says.

While Karen loves that cozy feel and nostalgic

smell of the store, she's also aware that there might be more of the store's past lingering in the shadows.

One of her former employees, Grace, was once closing up the store when she noticed something out of the corner of her eye. She absolutely knew that she was alone, but she was certain that she saw a little girl wearing old-fashioned clothing. The girl had long dark hair and brown eyes. She made a face like she was scared and then vanished in a flash. At first, Grace was worried that someone had left a child alone in the store, but then she realized the spookier truth. She was alone, there was no child, but there was very possibly a ghost.

Grace isn't the only person who has felt or seen the presence of a child. Another employee, Doris, heard a child crying when she was all alone in the store. She checked all around inside and outside the store. While she was absolutely convinced that the crying was coming from inside the store, she couldn't find any evidence that someone was in the building with her.

Doris also felt a cold spot upstairs, something several employees have felt over the years. As she walked past the counter, she felt a freezing cold spot. She was so afraid, she just kept on walking and headed down the stairs. She had no explanation for that moment of cold. The air conditioner wasn't on. There wasn't an open window nearby blowing in cold air. It was absolutely inexplicable and chilling.

Madeline, a current employee at the store, has also felt a cold spot in the store. Just like Doris, she couldn't find an explanation for the brief cold moment. It happened so fast. She also sometimes finds books thrown all around the upstairs room—a room she knows to be perfectly neat and tidy when she left it the night before.

While some might be scared by the unexplained mess, Madeline believes it's the work of a mischievous spirit. Over fourteen years at the store, she's only witnessed signs of ghosts three or four times—and that's not enough to scare her. (When she tells people the story, she laughs.)

What would you do if you worked at a haunted general store? Would you stick around after your first ghostly encounter? Would you find it funny, like Madeline did? Or would you walk out and never return?

CHAPTER 5

The Fire Island Lighthouse

FIRE ISLAND

Could the Fire Island Lighthouse be haunted? If you ask one of the lighthouse volunteers, they'd probably say no. But rumors of ghosts rumble through the lighthouse's history.

The current Fire Island Lighthouse is actually the second lighthouse to stand on Fire Island. The first lighthouse was built in 1827. For more than twenty years, it served as a guide for transatlantic ships, commercial fishermen, and boaters. Over time, however, the keepers realized that the lighthouse needed to be taller. It also needed to be built from more resilient materials that would stand up to the saltwater and wind.

That new lighthouse was completed in 1858. It stood seven stories high (at 168 feet), and its light was now visible for at least twenty-one miles. In 1973, the lighthouse was replaced by an electric strobe light. After 150 years serving sailors and seamen, the Fire Island Lighthouse was abandoned. It fell into disrepair until it was saved and preserved in 1982 by a group of concerned citizens.

During its years of service, the lighthouse saw its share of history from shipwrecks to hurricanes to pirates. One of the more famous shipwrecks occurred in July 1850 when the captain of the five-hundred-ton ship *Elizabeth* mistook the Fire Island Lighthouse for the Cape May (New Jersey) Lighthouse. The enormous ship violently crashed along the south shore of Long Island, leaving ten people dead. Among the dead were the famous writer Margaret Fuller, along with her husband and son.

In April 1950, a 432-foot freighter called the SS *Hurricane* hit a sandbar while traveling in the fog. It landed off Fire Island near the lighthouse. The ship was stranded there for thirteen days, and it took tugboats to finally pull it off the beach and back onto the water.

Not all shipwrecks involved such enormous boats. Sometimes, if smaller boats were destroyed in the middle of the night, the lighthouse keeper would wake up to cargo, pieces of ships, and even bodies washed up all along the shore. A haunting way to start the morning off, for sure.

Throughout history, pirates also took advantage of shipwrecks or, even worse, caused them. Pirates were known to light fires on the shores in order to confuse ship captains. The ships would sail toward the light and run aground, and then the pirates would rush aboard to steal all the valuables. (Some say this is how Fire Island got its name.) Pirates would also keep an eye on the shore, stealing whatever might wash up after a wreck. They were so ruthless, they'd sometimes steal cargo from the rescue ships sent to help damaged boats.

While these true tales of pirates and shipwrecks are haunting, it's the story of a father and his daughter that led some to believe the lighthouse itself is haunted.

Back when the new lighthouse was being built, the lighthouse keeper, his wife, and their daughter were forced to move temporarily into a new home. The lighthouse keeper was very upset about the move because the new home was cold and damp and his daughter was very ill.

As the days went on, the daughter's condition got worse. She developed a fever, and a doctor was called in from the mainland. Back in the 1800s, it wasn't simple to get a doctor out to isolated Fire Island, and the keeper and his wife waited three whole days for the doctor to arrive.

While anxiously waiting, the father climbed up and down and up and down the steps of the lighthouse—182 steps each way—hoping to catch a glimpse of the doctor as he arrived.

Tragically, the doctor didn't arrive in time, and the little girl died. With nowhere to bury her on the rocky shores of Fire Island, the girl was cremated in the fireplace.

Many believe that the clangs and bangs sometimes heard at the lighthouse are the heavy steps of the father walking up and down the steep staircase at night, waiting and waiting and waiting for the doctor who arrived too late.

OHEKA Castle

COLD SPRING HILLS

High up in Cold Spring Hills sits OHEKA Castle. (Yes! There's a castle on Long Island.) It's a castle full of cool details—secret rooms, cavernous libraries, a fascinating history, and ghost sightings.

OHEKA Castle was built by Otto Herman Kahn. Very proud of the castle, Otto named it after himself: **O**tto **He**rmann **Ka**hn.

Otto Kahn was born in 1867 into a wealthy banking family in Germany. At an early age, he found that he also loved working in banking. He worked in London for many years, and thought

London was fantastic. He loved it so much that he became a London citizen. But as time went on, Otto was intrigued by the idea of living in the United States. In 1893, he sailed to America to work for a banking firm in New York City.

Within just three short years, Otto became very successful. He married Addie Wolff, and they soon settled down in a beautiful mansion about an hour from New York City, in Morristown, New Jersey. Together, the Kahns traveled the world shopping for furniture, art, and antiques for their new home.

Tragedy struck in 1905 when a fire broke out and destroyed over $75,000 worth of furnishings and belongings. (That would be like losing over $2 million in chairs and curtains and other fancy things today.) Not surprisingly, Otto Kahn became very afraid of fire. While the family home was rebuilt, the Kahns started to realize that they weren't very happy in their

new town. Among other things, Otto was discriminated against because he was Jewish. Even with a beautiful home, life in New Jersey wasn't making the Kahns very happy.

As the years went on, Otto spent less and less time in Morristown. He bought homes in other states and eventually decided to settle down on Long Island. During that time, Otto befriended President Theodore Roosevelt and went on to become a US citizen.

In 1914, Otto purchased over 440 acres of land in Cold Spring Hills. His dream was to build an extraordinary French chateau on the highest point of Long Island. Unfortunately, someone already owned the highest point. So Otto spent two years carting in enough dirt to make a bigger hill. All in all, it took five years for his vision to be complete. The mansion was finally finished in 1919, and what a mansion it was! There were over 126 rooms and 109,000 square feet of living space. It was HUGE. In fact it was—and still is—the second largest private home in the United States (only the Biltmore estate in North Carolina is larger). Outdoors, there were gorgeous gardens, a greenhouse, an 18-hole golf course, horse stables, and even a private airstrip.

OHEKA castle was built in the style of a French chateau with lots of ornamental architecture like spires and steeply pitched roofs. French chateaus are also famous for beautiful woodwork. But remember Otto's fear of fire? He had his gorgeous library made of fireproof materials and then *painted* it to look like wood. Smart, right?

Another feature of French chateaus are secret tunnels and passageways. Otto definitely wanted some of those.

We know for sure that Otto's secretary had a private office that could only be entered through a revolving bookcase. That had to be a pretty cool way to go to work every morning.

There were also rumors that Otto had secret tunnels built in the house that ran to the harbor and the train station. While there's no way to confirm if that's true, a later occupant of the building, the Eastern Military Academy, did close up some tunnels during its time in the castle.

And here's an even more exciting rumor: some said that in the basement of the castle, Otto kept lions and tigers in enormous cages to protect the property. (While that's a fabulous story, it's more likely that the spaces in the basement were there to help cool down the house in the days before air conditioning.)

In 1934, Otto died of a heart attack in his office. He was only 67 years old.

Could it be that Otto still haunts the rooms of OHEKA, the home he loved so dearly?

Through the years, staff have had strange encounters in the castle. One of the castle's most popular rooms is the Charlie Chaplin room, which has been a site of many of these encounters. Charlie Chaplin was a hugely popular and important movie star during the silent movie era. Otto was a fan and a friend of Chaplin, so the current owner of the castle decorated a room in OHEKA with photos and other Chaplin memorabilia.

It's in that room that many visitors have reported seeing shadow people—dark shadows in the general shape of a person—or feeling like someone else was in the room even though they were alone.

People have also reported seeing a woman in the library, along with fleeting figures and creaking doors. Most haven't reported feeling anything scary or menacing about these encounters, just the sense that someone was there, keeping watch over the rooms.

One of the most confounding encounters happened to a caretaker named Scott Bellando. Scott worked at OHEKA for years. One night, he heard beautiful music coming from the piano on the first floor. He was certain he was the only person in the building. As the caretaker, he was the only one who had access to the building. But the music continued to get louder and louder. Whoever was playing the piano was good, too.

As the music swelled, Scott went to investigate. When he opened the door to the first floor, the music abruptly stopped. He walked toward the piano—and the bench was empty. The room was empty. He was all alone, now in silence.

Today, if you dare, you can visit OHEKA Castle with your family and see for yourself if Otto still presides over his castle, nearly 100 years after his death.

CHAPTER 7

Ketcham Inn

CENTER MORICHES

Bert Seides found one small child-sized shoe under the floorboard of the Ketcham Inn. One single tiny shoe. And not just an ordinary shoe, but a very, very, very old one. What could it mean? Who left it behind? Did that person—or their spirit—still linger at the inn? Let's look back at how the inn came to be.

Benjamin Havens ran an inn and tavern in Moriches during the American Revolution, when Long Island was under British occupation. In 1772, Havens proposed a stagecoach route that ran from Brooklyn all the way to Sag Harbor, passing through Moriches. As he had hoped, it seriously increased business at the inn.

In 1791, the inn was purchased by William Terry. He renamed the inn Terry's Hotel, and the Terry family went on to run it for over sixty years. The inn continued to get many visitors, even a few famous people, including Thomas Jefferson and James Madison.

In 1852, the hotel was sold to a man from Huntington, Andrew Ketcham. During that period, the hotel served many important purposes for the community. It was a local court as well as a voting station for local elections. During the Civil War, in the 1860s, volunteers came to the grounds to practice drills. The Ketcham Inn, as it was now known, served as a hub for the people of Center Moriches and everyone traveling the popular stagecoach route across Long Island.

Over time, the property continued to change hands and functions. At times, it's been a tearoom, a restaurant, and a shelter for women and children.

During the time the Ketcham Inn was a shelter, a terrible accident happened. A child playing with matches caused a fire. While no one was hurt, the building suffered serious damage.

That's when Bertram Seides, president of the Ketcham Inn Foundation, swung into action. Bert was the son of a local farmer, and he was very taken by the Ketcham Inn. A few years before the fire, the building had been for sale, and he'd visited it. He felt a strong connection to the place. When the fire happened, he was devastated and decided to do something about it. He eventually found a way to protect and preserve the inn.

Today, a small portion of the inn can be visited by the public while the rest of the building is being restored. Bert also opened up a small bookstore store on the property, the Book Barn, and the sales of used books help pay for the renovation and upkeep.

What about the single shoe that Bert found under the floorboards? It turns out that hiding shoes under the floor was something early settlers did to ward off bad spirits. The legend said that the shoe protected the owners of the house and offered good fortune. Generally, a shoe would be hidden near a point of entry in the home. In this case, the shoe was hidden near the chimney, an obvious entry point for evil forces (or so they say).

In truth, the hidden shoe is the least worrisome tale connected to the Ketcham Inn.

Many have heard a sadder tale about the tragic death of a young girl who died in the house. In preparation for her sister's wedding, chickens were being plucked and prepared for a feast. The little girl was playing with the discarded feathers when she got too close to the fire. The feathers caught fire, and then her clothes caught fire. She perished in the flames.

A psychic once visited the inn and saw the spirit of a young girl with long hair, possibly the child who died. She wasn't an angry spirit; in fact, she was pleased that they were working to restore the inn. Others have said they captured the girl ghost on film, with her apparition appearing in an upstairs window.

While the story of the little girl is the most haunting tale of the Ketcham Inn, other strange occurrences have happened over the years. One woman who lived in the house with her family from 1946 to 1955 remembers her father telling the tale of the mysterious latches that would open and close by an unseen hand. He would experience a feeling of terrible sorrow before hearing or watching the latches click open. She claims he never shook the experience, even long after they moved, forever haunted by the unexplainable event.

With so many stories and so many people coming through the doors of the Ketcham Inn, it seems more than possible that a few spirits have chosen to stick around.

CHAPTER 8

The Culper Spy Ring

Long Island was home to an amazing group of spies during the American Revolution. They used their wits, invisible ink, disguises, and even laundry hung out to dry to thwart the British in one of the most fascinating pieces of Long Island history—a piece of history that was ALMOST lost to the ages.

At the time the Declaration of Independence was signed, in 1776, the British (also known as the redcoats, because of their red uniforms) had a large army in America. When the revolution broke out, those British troops commandeered—or took over—everything they could from people's homes and businesses to cemeteries and village greens. Even in the quiet little town of Setauket, the world was turned upside down with the arrival of the redcoats. The soldiers turned the Presbyterian church into a British fort. The pews in the church were knocked down to make stalls for horses, and the tombstones were used as building materials for barracks. Watching their town destroyed by the British was very hard for the people of Setauket.

Those who were against the British occupation were called Patriots. In time, a group of Patriot soldiers sailed over to Long Island from Connecticut to wage war against the British. In August 1777, the Battle of Setauket took place, but the Patriots were outnumbered. Their attempt to overtake the British soldiers failed.

But those Patriots were not ready to give up. They wanted their freedom.

With careful planning and effort, the Culper Spy Ring was put into place a year later. The ring lasted for a full six years without the British ever catching on. In fact, it was such a secret that it took over 150 years for people to find out about it! A historian stumbled upon the secrets of the ring in 1939. Now that's the sign of a really, really good spy ring!

How did they do it?

It all started when General George Washington asked his trusted aide, Colonel Benjamin Tallmadge, to start a network of spies on Long Island. Tallmadge was based in Connecticut but had grown up in Setauket.

He turned to some trusted friends, including twenty-five-year-old Robert Townsend, a merchant and Patriot from Oyster Bay. His family owned a house that had been taken over by the British during the occupation.

Robert Townsend secretly served his country during the Revolution by becoming one of General George Washington's chief spies. He worked under the codename "Culper Jr."

Robert was a terrific spy. One time he dressed up as a redcoat and went to New York City, where he talked with British soldiers over tea. After, he shared what he learned with General Washington by sending him a note written in invisible ink.

Another member of the spy ring was Austin Roe, a twenty-nine-year old tavern keeper from Setauket. His job was to carry messages from New York City to the spy ring in Setauket. He disguised himself as a country merchant and rode fifty-five miles on horseback several days a week. He made hundreds of journeys and never got caught.

The head spy was a man named Abraham Woodhull, a descendant of Richard Woodhull, one of the first settlers in Setauket. He ran a farm that became his base of operations. Most of the letters passed back and forth in the spy ring were

written by Abraham. His secret name was "Samuel Culper Sr." He, too, rode messages from Setauket to New York.

During his travels, Woodhull would learn what the British were doing, how many troops they had, where they were going, and lots of other important details. Like everyone else in the area, his house was occupied by British troops, so he needed to pass along all he learned without alerting the redcoats.

To do so, Woodhull had fellow spy Austin Roe bring his cows to pasture on his land. Austin then hid messages in the hollow of a tree. Woodhull would get them and pass them on to another spy, Caleb Brewster.

While Austin and Abraham traveled by horse, Caleb was a skilled seaman. He knew how to navigate Long Island's waters. He was a huge asset to the spy ring and General Washington.

Caleb and a small band of spies would travel across the Long Island Sound to ferry messages to Tallmadge in Connecticut. On the way back, Caleb was known to attack and capture British supply ships. He would burn anything that belonged to the British and take any supplies that would be useful to the Patriots.

The spy ring included one remarkable woman: Anna Smith Strong, codename "Nancy." Anna was married to Judge Selah Strong, and together, they had eight children.

The first way Anna helped the cause was by giving orders to Austin, so his trips to the city looked like they had a purpose. She would order fabric and dry goods to make it seem like his frequent trips were part of doing normal business.

But Anna also played an even more ingenious role within the ring. It was dangerous for Caleb to land his boat in the same spot each time he returned from his trips to Connecticut, so the spy ring organized six different possible landing spots for Caleb. But if he landed in a different spot each time, how would Abraham Woodhull find him? That's where "Nancy's Clothesline" came in.

So the legend goes, if a black petticoat was hanging on the line, it meant that Caleb was in town. The number of handkerchiefs hanging on the line would indicate in which spot he could be found. Through his spyglass, Woodhull could count the number of handkerchiefs on the line and know exactly where he could find Caleb.

While Anna's husband wasn't on the list of spies, it's assumed he was somehow involved. He was eventually accused of communicating with the enemy and thrown into one of the worst British prison ships, the *Jersey*.

Prison ships during this period in history were horrible. Diseases such as smallpox and yellow fever swept through the boats, killing thousands. With so many prisoners crammed on board, a stay on a prison ship was very often a death sentence.

Once again, Anna bravely came to the rescue. She begged for permission to board the ship and visit her husband. She rowed alone, in a boat filled with food. The British took the food and released

her husband, who then fled to Connecticut to hide until the war ended.

You can visit the graves of Anna and Selah in the St. George's Manor Cemetery today. Near the gravesites is where Anna kept her incredible clothesline.

Do the spirits of the soldiers and spies continue to haunt the woods of Setauket? Some say they've heard cannon fire there. Others have seen mysterious ghostly orbs appear in pictures of those history-filled woods. No matter what spirits remain, there's a rich spirit of history alive, thanks to the ingenious efforts of Washington's Long Island spies.

Glen Cove Mansion

GLEN COVE

Sometimes, no matter how many times a home changes hands, the original owners refuse to leave. In the case of the Glen Cove Mansion, the Pratt family just can't move on.

Charles Pratt was born in 1830 and came to Glen Cove around 1890. He was a pioneer of the US petroleum industry and also a philanthropist—someone who uses his wealth to support good causes.

Pratt wanted to build a summer home on Long Island's Gold Coast—the area along the north shore where lots of wealthy people had estates. He eventually found a plot of land in the northern part of Glen Cove. He bought all 1,100 acres with a plan to build homes for himself and his children.

Unfortunately, not long after he purchased the property, Charles Pratt died. He had been living in a home called Manor House. When Pratt died, his wife remained in that home. Even after the other Pratt houses were built, the Manor House served as the center of their family life. When Mrs. Pratt died, her son John Teale Pratt lived in the house for a while until he had it taken down so he could rebuild his own home on the same site.

John lived in that new house—an elegant place with an Olympic-sized pool—until his death in 1927. His widow, Ruth Baker Pratt, lived there until her death in 1965.

Now known as the Glen Cove Mansion, the staff of the building are certain that the property is haunted. They believe it's the ghost of Ruth that haunts her beloved family home.

Over the years, many guests have reported sightings of an old woman with grey hair sitting quietly in the servants' wing, smiling. The people who claim to have seen this apparition have had no idea of the building's history, but their experiences are all remarkably similar.

Another former employee remembers closing up the bar when she saw a woman dressed in all white walk past. She said, "Excuse me, ma'am, the bar is closed," but the figure never stopped; she kept walking and then vanished into the night.

When the unexplained has happened over the years—a faucet turning on and off mysteriously, an unexplained whoosh coming through the fireplace—the staff would blame Mrs. Pratt.

While sightings of Mrs. Pratt have been the most frequent, there have also been sightings of a ghostly gentleman and cases where staff or guests see shadow people—a dark shadow—or have that feeling that someone else is in the room when no one there.

Today, the home is a venue for weddings and conferences. It's even been used as a film set. And each year, descendants from the Pratt family get together for a yearly visit to the home.

If Mrs. Pratt is here, why would she ever want to leave?

Winfield Hall

GLEN COVE

Winfield Hall was built in 1916 for Frank W. Woolworth. Woolworth was a multimillionaire who came from a poor family but grew up to be a hugely successful businessman. He owned the famous chain of variety stores called Woolworth's. These types of stores were known as five-and-dimes and sold candy, small toys, and lots of household items, all at very affordable prices. Some also had a lunch counter where you could sit and get something to eat. Woolworth's popped up all over the country, making Frank

Woolworth a very wealthy man. His dream was to own a magnificent estate on Long Island.

In the early 1900s, his dream came true when he bought a large piece of property in Glen Cove. On the property was a mansion, and he lived there with his wife until it was destroyed by fire in 1916.

Woolworth decided to rebuild in a big way. He spent over $9 million on a unique marble palace, making it one of the most expensive homes ever built. Just the marble staircase alone cost $2 million!

The house contained fifty-six rooms on three floors. Everything was beautiful, intricate, and expensive. The rooms upstairs were each unique and named for famous people in European history. There was a Napoleon room, an Elizabethan room, a Louis XVI room, and a Marie Antoinette room.

Outside the mansion, there was a sixteen-car garage, a decorative pool, marble Roman statues, a greenhouse, and formal gardens.

After the Woolworths died, the house was closed up for many years. The next owners, the Reynoldses, kept almost everything exactly as the Woolworths had left it—with two notable exceptions. First, Mrs. Reynolds permanently closed off the Marie Antoinette room because it was always cold in there. Second, the sixteen-car garage was converted into a laboratory where Mr. Reynolds first created aluminum foil. (Yes, these Reynoldses invented Reynolds Wrap!)

Eventually, sometime after Mr. Reynolds died, Mrs. Reynolds couldn't keep up with owning such a large home. She sold it to the Grace Downs School for Girls. It's at this time that strange things started to happen in the house. A cook from the school claimed to have seen the apparition of a young girl in the gardens, and many of the girls attending the school claimed to have seen a girl wearing a faded blue dress.

The Marie Antoinette room remained boarded up and locked, but some of the girls couldn't resist sneaking in. Once, a girl smuggled her boyfriend into the house using a secret doorway adjoining the locked room. Later that night, she woke up to see a woman wearing a blue dress, crying at the foot of her bed. The ghostly woman told the girl that soon she'd be joining her. Just two months later, that same girl was killed in an accident near the house.

A secretary who worked at the school also was given an upsetting message from a similar ghost. Two weeks later, she too suddenly died.

Maybe Mrs. Reynolds wasn't wrong to lock up such a terrible room.

In 1975, the school closed down and the house was sold. The new owners often heard sounds during the night—sobbing, murmurs, and whispers. There were also reports of a mysterious swinging chandelier, a general coldness in the house, and a feeling of being unwelcome.

A friend of the owners—who was also a psychic—came to visit. She believed that the house was haunted by Mr. Woolworth himself. She said it seemed like he was unwilling to give up his earthly possessions.

Today, the building stands in disrepair after a fire blazed through the property in 2015. Do the ghosts still walk the halls? Did the bad luck of the Marie Antoinette room cause the fire? Does Mr. Woolworth still roam, overseeing all the work he put into his mansion? Perhaps the next owners of Winfield Hall will learn the truth.

CHAPTER 11

William Sidney Mount

STONY BROOK

William Sidney Mount was born on November 26, 1807, in Setauket. He went on to become a famous American painter who captured scenes of everyday life. Mount was also an inventor who loved to fish, hunt, walk, and sail—all of which he could do in his own backyard.

Instead of having a traditional artist's studio, Mount invented a studio-on-wheels. It was a horse-drawn cart equipped with a stove, ventilator, window, and skylight. This meant he could work on his art at home or on the road.

Early in his career, Mount was fascinated with death, ghosts, and the supernatural. No one knows exactly why. Maybe he had a supernatural encounter? He once wrote in a diary entry, "It is true spirits can and do communicate with mortals, and all cases evince a desire to elevate or progress the Spirits of those with whom they are in communion." That sounds like he thought ghosts were good things—that they are here to help us.

Mount also used to attend séances at a friend's house in New York City. During one séance, he believed that the playwright Ben Jonson (from the late 1500s and early 1600s) came through. The scene sounds incredible. Supposedly, the center of the table kept moving and letters and pencils were moved around by invisible hands. Mount believed his foot was held by a spirit, and others in attendance felt their hands grabbed by a cold spirit hand. Those in attendance heard strange noises and felt unexplained touches throughout the séance too.

Mount believed that he received professional guidance from beyond the grave from the famous Dutch painter Rembrandt, who died in 1669. Apparently, Rembrandt channeled thoughts into letters that a psychic would "write" and then pass

along to Mount. According to Rembrandt, Mount was a fantastic painter, the best in the country! I suppose it's a good thing to have a ghost on your side. Rembrandt did also offer advice to Mount about his painting style and choice of subjects.

Over time, Mount backed down from his belief in the spirit world. But the spirit world seems to have stuck around Mount's old farmhouse.

Is it Mount himself who haunts his farmhouse today? Perhaps. While many who have entered the home have had supernatural encounters, it turns out that Mount is only *one* of several possible ghosts tied to the historic property.

Who else might be haunting the Mount house? Some believe it's Mount's first cousin Elizabeth.

In the 1960s, a family moved into the Mount house. Their daughter Elizabeth wasn't happy about the move. One night shortly after moving in, she swore that a woman dressed all in white appeared at the foot of the bed. The woman in white said that her name was Elizabeth too, and she welcomed the girl into the home.

The parents believed that Elizabeth was just dreaming. Was she? How could she have known that another Elizabeth was connected with the home? And why, after Elizabeth's encounter with the ghost, did the faucets start mysteriously turning on and off? Over the years, other family members saw figures in Revolutionary War uniforms and a woman in an old-fashioned blue dress.

Seems the William Sidney Mount house is haunted, no? Perhaps it was William's own interest in the supernatural that makes the home extra inviting for spirits. But even if the house is not filled with ghosts, it's most definitely filled with history and tales of the incredible life of the talented and eccentric William Sidney Mount.

CHAPTER 12

Lloyd Antiques

EASTPORT

When you think of places that might be haunted, antique shops are high up on the list. They're full of fascinating objects with ties to the past—paintings in heavy, old frames featuring long-dead people; much-loved jewelry from long ago that hung on the necks and ears and wrists of nineteenth-century ladies; dusty, leather-bound books with crinkly pages that smell like mushrooms; and a million flower vases from times gone by.

Who's to say that spirits won't come back to

visit their most beloved earthly possessions?

In Eastport, you'll find just such a wonderful antique shop brimming with interesting and unusual items from the past. But the ghost inside? He has an unusual and unexpected story.

Lloyd Gerard has always been a skeptic—someone who doesn't believe in ghosts. But even he admits that his store is haunted. As Lloyd himself says, "What I see, what I hear, what I smell—I have to believe, skeptic or not."

Strangely, the ghost in the antique shop is not connected to any of the items for sale. But he *is* very personally connected to Lloyd. It's Lloyd's great-great-great-great-uncle Levi. (Yes, four "greats.")

Andrew Simon Levi came to Long Island all the way from Russia in 1860. He was a teenager and wanted to avoid serving in the Russian army. Once he landed safely in America, he needed to find work. He became a traveling salesman, selling sewing needles door to door. Family history says he walked for two months to gather supplies, from Brooklyn to Montauk to Greenport to Orient and then back to New York City.

Uncle Levi was a hard worker who never married. He was a practical joker and a cigar smoker. After working hard his whole life, he died in 1926.

As Lloyd discovered by accident, Levi was buried in a potter's field in Patchogue, Long Island. A potter's field is where people are buried when they have no family, friends, or money. Levi came from a big, loving family. So how did he end up buried there?

That is exactly the reason Lloyd believes Uncle Levi came back to haunt him.

"My theory is that Levi is still here because he's annoyed," says Lloyd. "Nobody would pay for his funeral. He was their uncle. I don't think [he] had any money . . . his official cause of death was that *he just wore out*. Can you imagine that?"

All the relatives who knew Levi when he was alive are now dead. So Levi chooses to haunt Lloyd.

And while you might think Levi would be

angry after working a hard life and then landing alone in a potter's field, Lloyd thinks he's a fun and friendly spirit.

What exactly does Uncle Levi do to make his presence known at Lloyd Antiques? One tell-tale sign: cigar smoke. Uncle Levi loved smoking cigars, but Lloyd strictly forbids any of his employees or customers from smoking in the store. Still, many days, there's a strong smell of cigar smoke. When Lloyd smells it, he says, "It's Uncle Levi. He's here." Some have even seen a man smoking in the upstairs window of the store.

Another time, the ghost of Uncle Levi spoke with a customer and offered him a great deal on a table.

Says Lloyd, "He told [him] that a table upstairs was $65. It was a $400 table!"

Uncle Levi is also known to tip over tables and knock things off shelves—not the most desirable habit in an antiques shop.

For now, Uncle Levi remains a local legend in Eastport. Kids come in looking for the ghost, and Lloyd gets lots of calls around Halloween.

But Uncle Levi works on his own schedule. Lloyd has some advice for the people who call: "I tell them Uncle Levi doesn't come out on command."

Country House Restaurant

STONY BROOK

In 1710, Obediah Davis built a home for his family in Stony Brook. Over the years, the house changed and expanded—rooms were added on, new owners came and went. Its purpose changed too. It was used as a stagecoach stop for many years, a Sunday school for the local church, and finally, a restaurant.

It's not a very remarkable story on the surface. Long Island is full of old houses. But, if you dare, let's step a little closer.

Is that a graveyard out there, in the woods behind the house (which is now the Country House Restaurant)? Rumors of a murder? A ghost, lingering within the walls since the 18th century? Things are definitely not always as simple as they seem.

Bob Willemstyn has worked at the Country House Restaurant for over thirty years, and in 2005, he became the owner.

He had heard rumors for many years that Country House was haunted. He understood why during his first week on the job. One of those nights, he felt a change in the air. Suddenly, it was very, very cold. And heavy.

He heard someone call his name. "Bob?"

He turned around. No one was there. He was alone.

Bob believes that was his very first encounter with the ghost of Annette Williamson. Who was Annette? Why do people like Bob believe she's haunting a Long Island restaurant?

While details are scarce, one thing is certain: young Annette Williamson and her family lived in the home that is now the Country House Restaurant. Their tombstones are located in the back property along with around fifty other graves.

It's believed that Annette was part of a family of Dutch settlers who lived on Long Island during the period of the American Revolution (the 1760s–1780s). The family also owned land in New Jersey, and at some point, they left Annette, as well as her younger brothers and sisters, in charge of the Long Island home and property. What happened next can never be certain.

What we do know is that the British came and took over the home (something common during this time in history). Because she didn't resist that occupation enough, so the story goes, the townspeople accused her and the family of being British loyalists. During those tumultuous times, such accusations led to terrible things. Annette and her family were murdered. Some believe that the remainder of the family, those who were off in New Jersey, were also murdered.

So that's why many feel that it's Annette's

ghost at the restaurant. Bob isn't the only one who has witnessed her spirit. Some restaurant staffers have seen candles relight themselves. Others have noticed a beautiful young woman staring out from the window. Customers have seen her, and children have even tried to follow her around the restaurant. People have also noticed that Annette has a fondness for music, turning the volume up when she's enjoying a particular selection of songs. Over the years, again and again, people have noticed mysterious flashes of light, a change in the air temperature, and strong scents of vanilla, smoke, perfume, and chocolate in the air, all of which they've attributed to Annette.

Despite Annette's tragic history, she's been a friendly ghost for the most part. Some people admit they've felt deep sadness after sensing her spirit, but nothing more than that.

And Bob? After spending so many years in the same space with Annette, he believes she has a fondness for him.

He's convinced that she's made a game of stealing his tie clip. And from time to time, he still hears her call his name. And that's a good thing, isn't it? If you're going to run a haunted restaurant, making peace with the ghost is a very good idea.

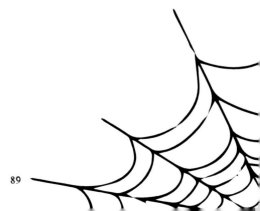

Biggs House

SETAUKET

The Thomas Biggs house was built sometime around 1680, and it stayed in the same family for over three hundred years. Its likely first occupant, Isaac Biggs, was one of the signers of the Articles of Association during the American Revolution.

Today, the house is owned by Therese and William "Bill" Brewster Seydel. (Get this: Bill is a descendant of Caleb Brewster, the famous spy from George Washington's Culper Spy Ring!) With all that history, it's no surprise that the Seydels believe the house to be haunted.

Therese had her first encounter with the Biggs's house ghosts when she was dating Bill. She saw a shadow in the mirror and assumed it was Bill's mom.

When she told Bill, he said that it was impossible—his mother was sleeping soundly upstairs.

Years later, after they married and had a young daughter, an even more chilling incident occurred.

"What are you looking at?" Therese asked her little girl, who was staring up at the ceiling.

"I wonder what the lady is doing?" replied her daughter.

Therese saw nothing. No lady, just the ceiling.

"That lady!" said her daughter, pointing at a spot on the ceiling.

Therese still saw nothing. She asked more questions. "What is she doing?"

Her daughter answered, "Looking for her babies."

After a few more questions, Therese learned that the woman's name was Sealy.

While some people might have immediately packed up and moved out of the house, Therese decided to investigate. Had a Sealy lived in the house before?

She asked around the neighborhood and learned that a woman named Sarah Ann Sells had lived in the neighborhood, just a mile away from the Biggs house, years before. She was a midwife and mother's helper, and she was known to be a very kind woman who handed out peanut butter and jelly sandwiches to the neighborhood kids. Her nickname? "Sarry"—not far at all from the name "Sealy" that Therese's daughter thought she heard.

Is it possible that 35 years after her death, Sarah Ann Sells came back to her hometown? Or was it all just a creepy coincidence that Therese's daughter thought she saw a woman named Sealy floating around the ceiling of the Biggs house?

CHAPTER 15

Villa Paul Restaurant

HAMPTON BAYS

Shadow people, ghost dogs, and a secret cemetery—these aren't things you'd normally find at an Italian restaurant. But at Villa Paul Restaurant in Hampton Bays, a haunting history offers diners a side of spooky with their spaghetti.

Villa Paul Restaurant didn't start off as a restaurant at all. In 1804, Phebe and Joseph Brown built a log cabin for their growing family. The home changed hands several times over the years, and in the early 1900s, it was purchased by the

CHAPTER 16

Raynham Hall

OYSTER BAY

Remember Robert Townsend (codename: Culper Jr.)? He was one of George Washington's chief spies in the infamous Culper Spy Ring, and it was his father who built Raynham Hall in Oyster Bay, back in 1740. It was a glorious old home with an ornate staircase that stayed in the family for several generations.

The first reported haunting of Raynham Hall can be traced back to 1930. An overnight guest staying at the home awoke to the sight of a ghostly white horse and rider outside her bedroom window. People believe it was the ghost of Major John André, a British officer who often visited the Townsend property during the American Revolution.

Whatever it was, I suspect that guest never came back to stay at the house again.

A second possible sighting of Major André happened in January 2000. At that point, Raynham Hall had been converted into a museum. A staffer who worked there claims to have seen a ghostly figure at the top of the home's Victorian staircase, wearing a waist-length blue jacket and only visible from the waist up.

A few months later, there was yet another possible sighting of the major, but this time he appeared downstairs. The person who saw him said he was "a sad-looking man in his late thirties, with dark brown hair . . . sideburns, and a drooping mustache." He walked across the hall then vanished.

If indeed the ghost of Major André was

haunting Raynham Hall, he was making no effort to keep his presence a secret.

Alas, it's rumored that the major isn't alone— other spirits have been seen over the years who definitely do not fit his description.

In 1999, a visitor walking past that same staircase heard the distinct sound of swishing skirts. When she turned, she saw a portion of a female figure dressed in Victorian clothing. The figure drifted past her and headed toward the back of the house.

In another incident, a staff member also claimed to have seen a black-caped form with a hood enter the pantry and the kitchen. Some believe this figure is the ghost of an Irish servant named Michael Conlin, who lived with the Townsends in the 1820s.

During a Halloween tour of the house in 2001, a guide told visitors the story of Conlin from the first floor of the house in an area that used to be the servants quarters. Suddenly, while the guide was speaking, the door slowly opened up and hit him in the hand. The guests all thought it was part of the tour—but the guide knew the truth. This was no gimmick.

Who opened that door? Could it have been the ghost of the former servant trying to play a Halloween trick on the guests?

With all these haunted sightings over the years, some ghost-hunting professionals have claimed that the hall and the staircase in Raynham Hall may be a ghostly vortex, or portal, that allows ghosts to enter into our world. Supposedly, many photographers have seen balls of light, known in ghostly terms as "orbs," when they develop their photos.

Whatever you believe, there's a long line of witnesses who claim to have seen or felt the spirits of ghosts inside Raynham Hall. Today, visitors can take tours of the space—including the hall and staircase. Is there a portal in that space? You be the judge.

So what do you think, are all these places on Long Island *really* haunted? There seem to be too many sightings and experiences to just say no, right? The history of Long Island is rich and full of amazing people and stories. Maybe you should visit some of these places on your own and experience them for yourself.

Rachel Kempster Barry is the author of *The Happy Book*, *This Book Is About You*, and several other titles about creativity, kindness, and being a helpful human. She grew up on Long Island, worked at Book Revue in Huntington, and loved visiting the Old Bethpage Village Restoration (she didn't see any ghosts on her visits, but she did love the candy in the General Store!). She lives in Madison, NJ, with her husband and cats.

Check out some of the other Spooky America titles available now!

Spooky America was adapted from the creeptastic Haunted America series for adults. Haunted America explores historical haunts in cities and regions across America. Original *Historic Haunts of Long Island* author Kerriann Flanagan Brosky has been working with medium and paranormal investigator Joe Giaquinto since 2005. She lectures around Long Island, and is currently at work on her ninth book. Here's more from Kerriann and Joe:

Haunted
Long Island
Mysteries
Coming
Soon

www.ghostsoflongisland.com
www.joegmediumpi.com